TESTIMONY: The Christian Writings & Testimonies of Arlin Ewald Nusbaum

TESTIMONY: THE CHRISTIAN WRITINGS & TESTIMONIES OF ARLIN EWALD NUSBAUM

ARLIN EWALD NUSBAUM

Alpha & Omega Publishing

https://lionandlamb.net

Ebook ISBN: 978-1-60135-986-5

Print ISBN: 978-1-60135-987-2

®

CONTENTS

INTRODUCTION

Some of Arlin's early testimonies were written when he was resigning from Mormonism 30 years ago and contain much of the Mormon vernacular. For Christians who would be offended or distracted by said mentions, Arlin has put his testimonies of Jesus here, using the Christian vernacular, and the Christian viewpoint.

To his previous readers, he would like to point out that there are many details that he did not include (even now he won't mention everything) because of their limited framework. For example, any administration from God is always composed of a "committee" of people, including overseers, helpers, and servants, which often comprise the faithful departed, different classes of angels, or other created beings.

When Arlin says a particular messenger was sent, it should never be assumed that the messenger was not accompanied by other committee members, whether to observe, take notes, assist, or in training for a future purpose of God.

The nature of other dimensions and spirit beings differs greatly from our limited mortal existence (though not entirely foreign to us). For example, it is possible for advanced spirit-beings to *know, monitor,* and *respond* to things that pertain to them *instantly.*

And as with our dream state (and the Veil of Faith), certain knowledge from divine encounters will be withheld from our conscious mind and released later. Knowledge is one of the great commodities of Heaven, and it is *highly regulated* for a variety of reasons.

Simply put, early in Arlin's life, he was shown in vision a list of books he would write one day. The *key* for unlocking the subject of each book, and for understanding it was woven into Arlin's "spiritual DNA" from before the foundations of this world and there was nothing he could do but faithfully bring forth each book which number over 100 along with 30 websites.

The stewardship of bringing particular knowledge to earth—at certain times—is what writers are doing. Once that knowledge has been brought to earth—to our human consciousness—it becomes available to everyone; for what one person comprehends, all can then comprehend. Just like backyard scientists whose inventions might not ever see the light of day, but their *ideas* could go on to revolutionize the world in some way, so also do the unlocked concepts that are brought to earth by inspired writers.

11 So shall my word be that goeth forth out of my mouth: it shall not return unto me void, but it shall accomplish that which I please, and it

shall prosper in the thing whereto I sent it. (Isaiah 55)

JESUS' EXAMPLE

Agony in the Garden by Frans Schwartz, 1898

Who was on Jesus' "committee" during his mortal sojourn? We know He was strengthened by angels, watched over closely by His Heavenly Father, and visited by at least two departed faithful—*Moses* and

Elijah. And weren't the words that Jesus was destined to bring to earth *already* prepared and authorized by God (or His committee)?

> 26 I have many things to say and to judge of you: but he that sent me is true; and **I speak to the world those things which I have heard of him**. 27 They understood not that he spake to them of the Father.
> 28 Then said Jesus unto them, When ye have lifted up the Son of man, then shall ye know that I am he, and that **I do nothing of myself; but as my Father hath taught me, I SPEAK THESE THINGS**.
> 29 And he that sent me is with me: the Father hath not left me alone; **for I do always those things that please him**. (John 8)

Jesus is also the *Spirit of Truth*:

> 12 I have yet many things to say unto you, but ye cannot bear them now.
> 13 Howbeit when he, **the SPIRIT OF TRUTH**, is come, **he will guide you into all truth**: for **HE SHALL NOT SPEAK OF HIMSELF**; but whatsoever he shall hear, that shall he speak: and he will shew you things to come.
> 14 He shall glorify me: for he shall receive of mine, and shall shew it unto you. (John 16)

> 16 And I will pray the Father, and he shall give you **another Comforter**, that he may abide with you for ever;

17 **Even the SPIRIT OF TRUTH**; whom the world cannot receive, because it seeth him not, neither knoweth him: but ye know him; for **HE DWELLETH WITH YOU, and shall be in you.**
18 **I will not leave you comfortless: I WILL COME TO YOU.** (John 14)

BURDEN OF PROOF ON RECEIVERS

The burden of receiving God's sent Word today is upon the hearer or reader:

40 **He that RECEIVETH you [those sent] RECEIVETH me**, and he that receiveth me receiveth him that sent me. (Matthew 10)

If God had prophets anciently, why can't He have them today? The question here is: "Does God speak today like He did anciently?" And "Is God the same yesterday, today, and forever?" (Hebrews 13:8) Does God have nothing more to say? Or does He not care about the situations we are in? The answer is: God IS the same, and He is not done speaking to His children. He cares about the situations we are in—*especially about the divisions among Believers.*

Believers today will be tested to see if they will reject God's prophets like His people did anciently.

20 Verily, verily, I say unto you, **He that receiveth WHOMSOEVER I SEND receiveth me**; and he that receiveth me **receiveth him that sent me.** (John 13)

6 We are of God: **he that knoweth God heareth us**; he that is not of God heareth not us. Hereby know we the spirit of truth, and the spirit of error. (1 John 4)

WHAT IS THEIR PURPOSE TODAY?

Modern prophets are to reprove the world of sin for not believing in Jesus, and to Believers for not putting into practice the things that Jesus *alone* taught:

7 Nevertheless I tell you the truth; It is expedient for you that I go away: for if I go not away, the Comforter will not come unto you; but if I depart, I will send him unto you.
8 And when he is come, **he will reprove the world of sin**, and **of righteousness**, and **of judgment**:
9 Of **sin, because they believe not on me**;
10 Of **righteousness,** because I go to my Father, and ye see me no more;
11 Of **judgment, because the prince of this world is judged**. (John 16)

7 But in fact, it is best for you that I go away, because if I don't, the Advocate won't come. If I do go away, then I will send him to you.
8 And when he comes, he will convict the world of its sin, and of God's righteousness, and of the coming judgment.
9 The world's sin is that it refuses to believe in me.

10 Righteousness is available because I go to the Father, and you will see me no more.

11 Judgment will come because the ruler of this world has already been judged. (John 16 NLT)

10 And **now also the axe is laid unto the root of the trees**: therefore every tree which bringeth not forth good fruit is hewn down, and cast into the fire.

11 I indeed baptize you with water unto repentance: but he that cometh after me is mightier than I, whose shoes I am not worthy to bear: **he shall baptize you with the Holy Ghost, and with fire**:

12 Whose fan is in his hand, and **he will throughly purge his floor**, and gather his wheat into the garner; but he will burn up the chaff with unquenchable fire. (Matthew 3)

14 Now **therefore fear the Lord**, and serve him in sincerity and in truth: and **put away the gods which your fathers served** on the other side of the flood, and in Egypt; and **serve ye the Lord.**

15 And if it seem evil unto you to serve the Lord, **CHOOSE YOU THIS DAY WHOM YE WILL SERVE...but as for me and my house, we will serve the Lord.** (Joshua 24)

Trail in Nazareth

Details of that trail in Nazareth are not given here, but can be found in my *TESTIMONY: Land of the Master*, 2022.

CHAPTER 1.

PROFILE OF A PROPHET

Arlin, Almond Orchard, 2002

Some people who have read my books are wondering just how a person could have so many profound experiences. My hope with this title is to remove any mystery that readers may have regarding Heavenly encounters. Often when we read about experiences in scripture, we are inclined to classify them as historical or mysterious. Consequently, readers may be inclined to judge God as being the sole instigator of such things.

These views, however, remove personal involvement for facilitating said encounters, and the reader is left to assume God does the choosing and they don't need to do anything.

In my walk with God, I have learned that this is not the case. Our lives are all heading down a certain path, in a certain way, but nothing is set in stone. If it were, there would be no need for either God, angels, or a Savior. God enjoys growth. He enjoys helping those who want to move forward, and He will appoint angels to assist them as they do so.

I believe God sows seeds in our hearts all the time (just as in *The Parable of the Sower*, Matthew 13:3) and some seeds take hold, and some don't. If we want to call *that entire process* mysterious, or the point where God does the choosing, then I guess that would be accurate. But that is all. What comes to bear fruit after the sowing is nothing but the result of our *personal hard work*.

Those who have done missionary service are aware that to find someone to teach or help, we must look, and God's Spirit will never lead us unless we ask. This process of asking is how it is with Heavenly encounters as well. For example, most people believe that the apostle Paul was an evil man, out to punish the Christians, and that God had to intervene. Actually, it was Saul who instigated the contact by a prayer *in his heart* for clarification (that's what he told me).

How do you make contact with God, Jesus, or ancient prophets? I am going to explain this so that the mystery will be replaced by an understanding of how God deals with humanity, and I will do that by characterizing who I am. For the first seventeen years of my life, I never had a Heavenly encounter. Though I was raised in Church, I can honestly say that I only felt God's Spirit three times, and the whisperings of The Holy Ghost twice.

I know of, and have heard about, others who had spiritual encounters as children, but such was not my fate. My first Heavenly encounter only came after *much prayer, faith,* and *fasting.* In fact, I know that it only happened after going through *trials of faith,* like Abraham. It was in the latter part of my sixteenth year that I decided to turn from my wicked ways, and to turn to God.

I recall paying a visit to the pastor to prepare for serving in the church. I took the occasion to confess my sins going back many years; he listened, then responded: "The Lord loves you very much and forgives you of all your sins." I believed what he said, *but in my heart,* I still felt as distant from God as before; I still felt a burden for the things I had done.

When I went away to college, I continued to try and align myself with God, and particularly to prepare myself spiritually for missionary service. I spent many days fasting, praying, and seeking the peace that only God could give. There on the floor of my dorm room one weekend while others were out partying, I went into deep communion with God (my prayers would often go for two or more hours). That's when I experienced my first Heavenly encounter.

As I was seeking God, He sent an angel; the Heavens opened to me, and I could see the angel coming from a great distance, from a Heavenly realm. As he came closer and closer, his glory and presence grew brighter and brighter. The wickedness of my past sins stood out like a sore thumb and I was spiritually undone. It quickly reached an intolerable state for me. I begged the angel to depart, and he did.

After that experience, I spent even more time in *prayer* and *fasting*, and in going on long hikes just to pour out my heart to God that He might rid me of my sins. I determined to visit a new pastor at college with the hope that if I confessed my sins to him, he might have a different approach. It was there in that pastor's office that I had my second Heavenly encounter, one that changed my life *forever*.

As I poured out my heart to this pastor, I cried many tears, for the nakedness of my past sins (as revealed by the recent angel encounter) magnified my willingness to rid myself of them all the more. This pastor differed from the first in how he handled the situation. He gave me a book to read, put me on a *repentance program*, and sent me to a more senior pastor for additional help.

The more senior pastor likewise gave me assignments with scriptures and other things to read. They both committed themselves to help me through my process of becoming spiritually clean. "It would not be easy," they each said, but, "It would be done properly." More than anything, I wanted my heart to be right with God.

It was now more than a year and a half since I had turned my life over to God and had begun the process of repenting of all my past sins. During that time there were many stages I went through, but finally I was at the most significant stage I would yet experience. It was there in the pastor's office during one of our meetings that Jesus revealed Himself to me.

He stood silently, dressed in a white robe, with His finger pressed to his lips, and He spoke to my mind the following:

I am aware of all of your efforts and will continue to monitor your progress.

I wanted so much to get out of my chair and run to Him, for He did not just radiate glory, but *compassion* and *love,* and I appreciated His *acknowledgment* of my efforts and His *encouragement.* This is how it has always been in my life. He (or angels) watches and I work, and sometimes He (or they) will acknowledge my efforts, or at other times He (or they) will teach or give instructions (I believe others are experiencing the same thing).

After having met Our Lord and being put on the road to *true* repentance by the help of these two pastors, I earnestly continued to purify myself. One thing that I took advantage of was access to old reel-to-reel sermons by some of the great preachers of our time, and I listened to those in the church's attic *repeatedly.*

I could not get enough of God's word, whether spoken or written. I distinctly recall the first time that I felt God's Spirit well-up in me while reading His holy Word. It did not come after the first sentence, or the first verse or chapter. It took me over 120 pages of intense reading (preaching, not history or genealogies) while being in a state of *hungering* and *thirsting* after righteousness before I felt God's confirming Holy Spirit.

I noticed it **came when I read** and **left when I stopped.** Each day I would experience this dynamic, and each day God's Spirit would stay with me a little longer than the day before, so long as I was intently reading powerful words of scripture. I was simply amazed by what I was experiencing. I wondered if this is how a person is supposed to feel all the time, or only on rare occasions?

I asked different church members and leaders, and I got different responses. What I experienced that day, and continue to experience until this time, is that God's Spirit will confirm His holy word. The more of it we take in, the more confirmations of God's Spirit we will receive. For example, I know that my soul was incompatible with God's Spirit at that time; it seemed like it was not welcome nor compatible with me.

Slowly, my thoughts and desires began to change, and my heart and mind were becoming fashioned in a new way, a way that was more compatible with His Spirit. I finally reached the point where I felt God's Spirit burning within my bosom *continually*. In fact, I always knew just how close I was to God (or how distant) depending on the degree of peace I felt.

For me, it was both *physical* and *spiritual*; God's Spirit affected both. What the apostles felt in their hearts on the road to Emmaus, I was feeling in my heart **all the time:**

32 And they said one to another, **Did not our heart burn within us**, while He talked with us by the way, and **while He opened to us the scriptures**? (Luke 24)

I learned through trial and error that it is up to each person how often they are in that state *if they are willing to do what is required.* Personally, I became very preoccupied with seeking God's Spirit after those two Heavenly encounters; **it was all I wanted to do, to know Jesus more, and to know how God's Spirit worked.**

From the time that I chose God at the end of my *sixteenth* year to when I was in the mission field at age *nineteen,* served entirely as a trial of my faith before God. Many of my friends who intended to go on missions failed. It was there on my mission in very humble circumstances that I finally received what I had been seeking for three long years—**the peace of God**—and that came **after** the Baptism of Fire:

16 John answered, saying unto them all, I indeed baptize you with water; but one mightier than I cometh, the latchet of whose shoes I am not worthy to unloose: **he shall baptize you with the Holy Ghost AND WITH FIRE** (Luke 3)

This event was most powerful; the process took *three days* and *three nights* to rid my vessel of past sins and their energy residue. After the process was completed, *I was a new person*. What began first with one pastor and then another, then with an angel, then with Jesus, then with those old reel-to-reel sermons by God's great preachers, and diligently reading God's Word faithfully, to making it out on my mission and being there willingly with all of my heart—then it came. That's how it was for me. Everyone's experience will be different.

My body could now handle a much larger concentration of the presence and power of God's Spirit, and many of its gifts became activated within me. For example, I could now see into the World of spirits. Often when teaching the Good News to a person, I might see an angel, deceased family member, or demons and their fallen cohorts.

But with that greater awareness came higher levels of *deception* and *distraction*. While girls, food, or other material things would be the predominating tempting force for missionaries, I was being tempted by rulers in high places to leave my mission, join other movements, become a healer, etc.

Throughout my life, I would see more and more

of this other dimension; it was a hard road to travel alone with no one instructing me or giving advice.

Arlin, Ocean Beach, Near Golden Gate Park, 1992

CHAPTER 2.

TESTIMONY OF THE SON OF GOD

I willingly share my testimony of Our Savior and who Our Savior is. The first thing the Lord wants me to do is to recount my most recent experience with Him, which was most profound. This will help others to know what is possible with their walk with Our Lord.

I recently finished a treatise that I was instructed to write by Our Lord called *My Walk With God* (follows this chapter). In it, I relate what I call the *Fire of Reliance*. These were the times in my life when I *learned* to rely on Our Lord. For some reason, Our Lord wanted me to reflect on those and document them. That discourse signaled the end of a *20-year revelatory experience with God*. I wrote many treatises during that time that deal with my journeys as I learned who God is, how His Spirit works, what state the Christian Church is in, etc.

The truth is, most people will never have a *need* that warrants a *personal* visit by Jesus. God the Father has many angels who can minister sufficiently well; Our Lord has given us His holy Word, and He does not respond to mere curiosities. Even for the truly sincere, He may refrain if they are not ready for a greater level of holiness.

Nevertheless, Jesus can personally administer to many people at the same time, and He regularly does so. Though He is far greater than us mere mortals, He respects all the Father's children, because we, too, are capable of greatness beyond all imagination. That is why Jesus will condescend to help any person who dares to ask.

For those who wonder if they can have a visitation of Our Savior, the answer is "Yes." But, *(a) it must serve a purpose; (b) it must be warranted; (c) the person must be capable of enduring some degree of His holiness;* and *(d) it must be approved by God the Father.* Without these things, any encounter for the sake of having one would inevitably be met with sure embarrassment. Not just for the individual, but for those watching.

My hope with this chapter is to help prepare others to meet Our Savior, and to avoid such embarrassments. He IS coming, and all must face Him one day, whether we initiate the contact. Now on to the experience that Jesus has asked that I share.

When I wrote the treatise *My Walk With God,* I was following Our Lord's instructions. The instructions began with *what* day we would meet and *where* we would meet. The leading of Our Lord was so strong that I knew I was destined to unite with Him and the Heavenly environment that He and His messengers bring with them.

I traveled high into the mountains (per His instructions) and arrived at a private lake; it was a beautiful day with no one around. As at other meetings, God shone a pillar of glory over the place I should stand. As I waited, Our Lord appeared; there was no one at this lake but us. With Him by my side, and with the Heavens opened overhead, I was truly basking in the light of God and His Son.

For me, this was a time for fellowshiping, for His glory, and the glory that came from above did not overwhelm me. Jesus then brought to my mind each of the previous times in my life that I chose to turn to God. I could see each scene from my past clearly displayed before me. Jesus was teaching me things about myself *from His perspective*. As He did so, my amazement was equal to His joy.

I know that each time that I turned to God, it meant the world to Him and Our Lord. Jesus loved me, and respected me for each of those times, and my confidence before Him grew (it is always humbling to be before Our Lord). There, under a clear blue mountain sky, I communed with Our Lord as two friends, and it was truly profound.

This was a milestone with God that I will probably only experience once, maybe twice, in this mortal life. I recognized I may never have another time of reflection as I did that day with Him. After the reflections were over, the sun was setting over the mountains, so I went to get some dinner and find a place to stay for the night.

Our Lord stayed with me and suggested we celebrate the day by renting some movies. As I looked through the movies, He prompted me with which two I should get. It was good to relax after such a long day of *driving, writing,* and *learning* (I had been fasting until then). It is hard for me to relay what I feel in the presence of Our Lord, but simply put, the environment changes, and *time and space is shifted.*

As always, this effect brings a sense of *other-worldliness* or *eternity* with it—how can it not! For that moment, in that location, Heaven merges with earth, and I look forward to the day when the *entire* world will merge with Heaven, so all can feel what I have enjoyed; it is entirely profound.

I then positioned two chairs in front of the TV, one for Jesus, and one for myself. Though He was with me for the duration of this excursion by His presence, it was not until after dinner when we sat together for the movies that Jesus *physically* sat next to me. Again, He was being the consummate gentleman, and was neither intimidating (not purposely, though He still is) nor trying to pacify me.

There we were, doing something that may only ever happen once, maybe twice in my life, enjoying each others fellowship at the end of a long and eventful day. The movies He prompted me to get I had never seen before, and both spoke of great integrity. One was called *Amistad* (and the other I will not name). No two movies could have been more appropriate for who I was with, for Jesus is a being of *utmost integrity.*

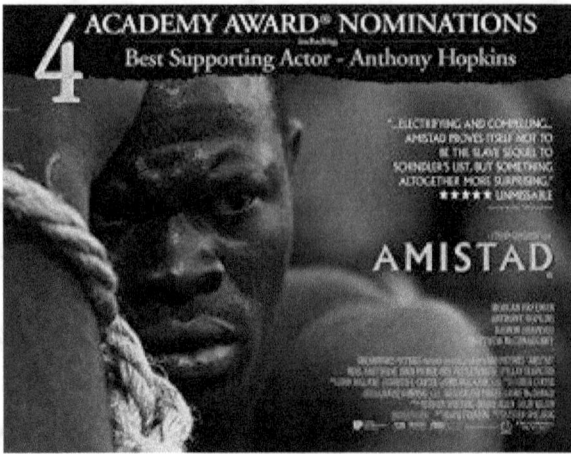

Amistad Movie Poster

These events are true, and Jesus did fellowship me. I did not seek it, but I certainly appreciated it. No, He did not let loose His amazing glory, nor did He seek to overwhelm me in any way, but was at all times very respectful of what would be most fitting for our *fellowshiping*, not *worshiping*.

Now let me tell you about the man, Jesus. First, we must understand that the reason His neighbors originally rejected Him was because He was a man. Which means, He had a face not everyone liked, a body type not everyone liked, and a host of other human traits you could easily judge.

Jesus is absolutely one with the present. He is an expert on current affairs. He is aware of all things and is easily part of them. You could not present a problem to Him He did not already know about, or that He did not fully understand. There is absolutely no situation He could not deal with successfully.

This is all that Our Lord would like me to share. It

is just one man's testimony of a time of fellowshiping with Jesus and I do not doubt that others have also experienced one-on-one time with Him. May I leave you with this promise from Our Lord:

20 Behold, **I** stand at the door, and knock; if any man hear my voice, and open the door, **I will come in to him**, and will sup with him, and he with me. (Revelation. 3)

Chi-Rho and Alpha & Omega Symbols

CHAPTER 3.

WALK WITH GOD

THE FIRE OF RELIANCE

The following describes the times when I was alone and had no one to turn to except God and God alone, and I know it's times like these that others have come to know Him as well. The first incident came when I was around fourteen years of age. Our family often went into the Rocky Mountains to camp, hike, and play. On this occasion, I went off on a motorcycle to the top of a mountain and then followed a trail until eventually I became lost.

I was on the shadow side of the mountain, and the sun was on its way down. It was getting cold, and I would soon run out of gas. So I began to desperately pray and ask for God's help. Suddenly, I came across someone who instructed me in the most direct way down to the main road, which I could then follow back to our campsite.

I began down a narrow, dirt, winding mountain road, turning the motorcycle off and coasting to save gas. I continued my prayers to God that I might make it down before dark and back to the campsite intact (I also had a river to cross to get to the road).

As I traveled down the mountain as fast as I could maneuver the motorcycle, I was suddenly warned by my guardian angel of imminent danger. His voice said to me, "Slow down, there's a gigantic snake around the next turn." Though I was desperate to make it back to camp and was going rather fast in order to beat the darkness, I gave heed and slowed down.

To my great surprise, around the next turn was indeed a huge, black snake, stretched right out across the entire width of the road. "Surely it heard and felt the vibrations of my motorcycle coming with the chain clanking and the brakes squeaking," I said to myself. So why was this thing lying there, completely stretched out across the full width of this road? I could not believe my eyes (the only snake I'd ever seen that large in diameter was a python brought by a snake handler to school).

At first, the snake did not move. Then, as if disappointed I stopped, it slithered off the edge of the narrow mountain road—where to I do not know for the side of the mountain dropped straight down. *In my moment of desperation*, the evil one morphed into a serpent and tried to take my life prematurely, for surely, if I would have gone over the side of that mountain, my life would have ended.

Since that day until now, I have been mindful that when we're all alone, *God is still there*; Jesus reminded me of that experience. The next opportunity to turn to God came at college, and I have already recounted part of that, but there was more. It was midterms, and I was getting overwhelmed, and it was showing in my grades. I shared that news with my dad and he questioned what the problem was: where was my time going he asked? Did I have a girlfriend? Was I partying?

I informed him that my time was solely divided between church, school, Bible classes and nothing more. He replied I had plenty of time to focus on those things *after* college, and to just focus on college now. I said I would rather die than forsake my interest in God, serving others, and learning His Word. I persisted in those interests which made for many sleepless nights, and I implored God to help my retention rate. Jesus said He remembered those prayers, and how challenging it was.

Another time Jesus reminded me of was prior to my mission service, after the school year had ended. I was working through the summer to save money for the mission, but wanted to take two weeks off just before leaving to prepare myself spiritually. My mother, however, was not too pleased with that idea and demanded that I work until my last day or that I should live somewhere else.

I just had to put God first, so I moved out. Unfortunately, my mother disowned me that day, but that's how rigid she was in her life. Jesus said He was mindful of that time and the decision I made, and what the cost was. All these memories were being shown to me in 3D, and I was also re-experiencing the emotions.

Next, Our Lord took me through my mission service and showed me the times I could have strayed as other missionaries had, but chose to place my service to Him and my fellow man first. There were too many examples to enumerate here, and some of these instances are too sacred or serious to share.

Perhaps the most significant time that I turned to God was when my first wife left me. She had been a convert for only one year when we married. I could have never guessed that she would turn to her old pursuits of fame in a music career at the expense of our marriage and her relationship with God. The last time she left me, we were living in America, and she took our two little children to the other side of the world (Australia) without my foreknowing.

The fabric of my life was *torn* from me; I loved those children dearly, and I loved her, but I could not compete with her Australian family or her interests in music and fame. Though I would try for the next *four years* to meet her every demand, everything failed; *those were very lonely years.* I worked two and often three jobs to make ends meet, and could not enjoy life whatsoever during that time.

She held me on a string tight enough to give me hope for the restoration of our family, but loose enough so she could do whatever she wanted in Australia and keep me at bay. I could not in good conscience go out with work associates, go to parties, go to sporting events, go on vacations, or do *anything* except try to mend a broken marriage and spend any spare time on the phone with my family.

Through it all, God was my only strength—He was all that I had. Only Jesus knew the pain that I endured for having my children torn from me when the mother never really wanted children. Those scenes were quite painful to relive, but I saw them from His view, and He comforted me.

From the time I left for college, until I married my soulmate, I had been single *and alone for seven years.* For details, see my wife's forthcoming book, *The Wife of a Prophet.* Those seven years taught me how to rely on God in very intense ways. *The Fire of Reliance* is to prove that you will turn to God in **every time of need**.

Had I not done so in every case, I would now be lacking those years of personal growth in my relationship with God. I can truly say:

> The Lord is my shepherd; I shall not want. He maketh me to lie down in green pastures: he leadeth me beside still waters. He restoreth my soul: he leadeth me in the paths of righteousness for his name's sake. Yea, though I walk through the valley of the shadow of death, I will fear no evil: for thou art with me; thy rod and thy staff they comfort me. Thou preparest a table before me in the presence of mine enemies: thou anointest my head with oil; my cup runneth over. Surely goodness and mercy shall follow me all the days of my life: and I will dwell in the house of the LORD for ever. (Psalms 23)

Perhaps readers can now appreciate how taxing and eventful the day was (as previously noted) and why the evening respite with Jesus was greatly needed and appreciated. He did not just take me through those remembrances and leave me on my own, but stayed with me, consoling, encouraging, and, most of all, fellowshiping.

I praise you God, and I thank you Lord Jesus, for your goodness, your kindness, and your enduring mercy.

Arlin, Almond Orchard, 2002

CHAPTER 4.

SERVICE

After my missionary service, I served as pastor for several churches, and I would like to mention two of those. The first was Assistant Pastor, that doubled as Youth Pastor. Many of the youth were fatherless, and as with every generation, those are challenging years. To do my part, I started a martial arts school and taught those classes at the church.

My life was quite full with a wife, full-time schooling, pastoral responsibilities, and martial arts classes. We lived in the country, and between travel time to get into the city and give the youth rides to and from church, plus fuel costs, it was taxing.

It was during one of our camping excursions after I had been laboring as described for some amount of time, while walking through the forest that, unexpectedly, Our Lord visited me. Like at other times, He wanted me to know that He (and others, for there was a whole host with Him) was aware of all my efforts and the sacrifices that were being made (I do not doubt that others have had similar experiences).

The second encounter was like the first and happened when I was called to serve at a different church as pastor over the men (ages 18 and up). Jesus visited me and said,

> Because you have been called to serve the men of this congregation (many husbands and fathers) you have direct access to my help on their behalf.

I believe *many* people in servant roles have received similar witnesses. As with all pastorships, there are plenty of opportunities to serve and to help. I helped more families move during that tenure than at any other time in my life.

Arlin, Missionary, 1982

CHAPTER 5.

TESTIMONY MEETING

Our Lord has commanded that I share an amazing event during my first year at college (Oklahoma University), back when I was intently seeking forgiveness and God's peace.

I shall never forget the rawness of being a first-year student in that new environment and being so hungry for God. After classes, I would go across the street to what was called "Institute," which was a building just for college students. They offered religious classes, and it was a place for students to hang out and take part in different activities.

Because this was a university, the spectrum of students ranged from the young 18-year-olds (like myself) to grad students who were in their 30s and 40s. The younger students dominated the building and classes during the day, with the older stopping in because it had good parking, and possibly to study, eat, or take an evening class.

Because of my hunger for God, I took day and evening classes and began to make friends with both age groups. Students who lived in the dorms were not provided food on weekends and so the Institute facilitated Sunday night dinners that all could attend, and this would bring in non-students, which was a good time to meet new people.

After the food, a service was held, which gave people the opportunity to introduce themselves and say a word or two if they wanted. No doubt many came with the sole purpose of seeing the latest crop of students for dating potential.

This experience happened early in the semester and I had not yet made many friends, and only a few of the locals. There was a *rawness* there, with so many unfamiliar faces, different age groups, and not everyone was a university student.

During this service, all it took was a few *heartfelt* expressions of one's love for God to open the environment for *everyone* to feel safe to express their struggles or sins, and those who had only just introduced themselves stood up again and opened up. And with every testimony, God's presence grew. Many tears were shed until every person got out everything that needed to be shared.

Two hours later, the meeting ended and everyone rose from their chairs, which were formed in a large circle, and went to each other weeping with joy, and the hugs and kisses could not be restrained. Word of this event spread near and far, and the older, more senior instructors who had seen students come and go by the thousands for decades said they had never witnessed anything like this; it was genuinely profound.

Many people came to Christ that night, and others

found their soulmates and later married. It was truly a blessed event and I have not been in a meeting that anointed since, and I have attended many spirit-filled events in the past 40 years.

Neither praise, worship, or unknown tongues brought in the presence of God that strongly; and not a single person broke out in unknown tongues. This is what is needed in the Body of Christ—*Reverential Holiness:*

> 7 **God is greatly to be feared** in the assembly of the saints, and **TO BE HAD IN REVERENCE** of all them that are about him. (Psalms 89)

> 28 Wherefore we receiving a kingdom which cannot be moved, **let us have grace**, whereby we may **SERVE GOD ACCEPTABLY WITH REVERENCE** and **godly fear** (Hebrews 12)

There are times for singing, praising, and dancing like David:

> 14 And **David DANCED** before the Lord **with all his might**; and David was girded with a linen ephod. (2 Samuel 6)

But what was the cause of his dancing?

> 14 And **David DANCED** before the Lord **with all his might**; and David was girded with a linen ephod.
> 15 So David and all the house of Israel **BROUGHT UP THE ARK OF THE LORD**

with **SHOUTING, and with the SOUND OF THE TRUMPET.** (2 Samuel 6)

Do we have the Ark today? And is there a single church or group that "brought up the ark into the city of David"? Then one might ask, how could "dancing like David" be justified? As it says in *Ecclesiastes*:

4 **A TIME** to **WEEP,** and **A TIME** to **LAUGH; A TIME** to **MOURN,** and **A TIME** to **DANCE;**
(Ecclesiastes 3)

But if that form of worship becomes the be-all and end-all, the deeper, more desirable Reverential Holiness will never come. I dare say, after 40 years of observing many forms of worship, Christians, by and large, are unfamiliar with the presence of God the Father.

Many are consumed and pre-occupied with signs, wonders, and speaking in unknown tongues, which is the administration of the Holy Ghost—they know it, they say and teach it, but what they don't know, and what they aren't teaching, is there's a **whole other spirit—the Spirit of God the Father**.

This is what was prophesied would come in *Joel 2* and other verses; not more of the Holy Ghost, this was confirmed and taught by Percy Collett, who spent eight days in Heaven where Jesus taught him this and other precious truths.

PERCY COLLETT's
Map of Heaven
by
Arlin Ewald Nusbaum

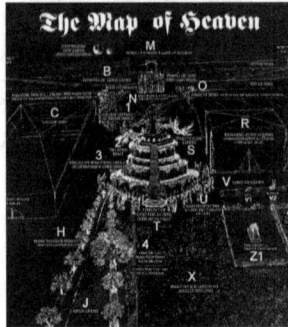

Percy Collett's Map of Heaven by Arlin Ewald Nusbaum

The following books go into detail about the fruit and misuse of tongues from firsthand experiences:

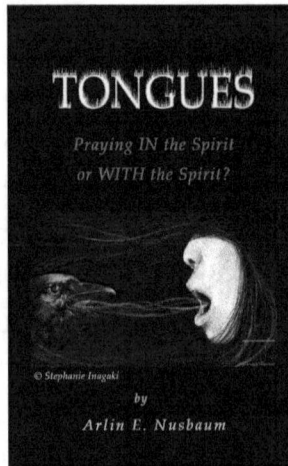

Tongues by Arlin E. Nusbaum

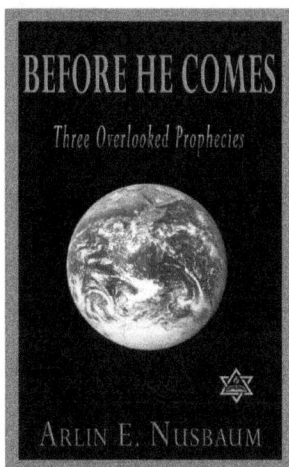

Before He Comes by Arlin E. Nusbaum

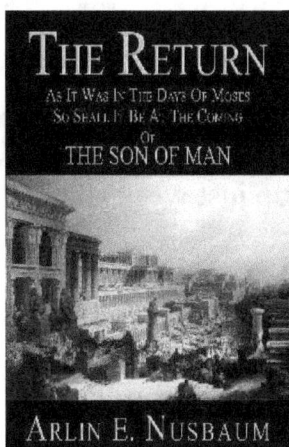

The Return – As It Was In The Days Of Moses by Arlin E. Nusbaum

CHAPTER 6.

INTO THE WILDERNESS

It was towards the end of this pastorship, while on one of my Prayer Hikes, that God the Father visited me by His Spirit and asked the following question:

If My Son came tomorrow, would you be ready?

When the Father or Jesus asks a question like this, they are essentially saying: "There is something we would like to unfold to you, but we can't do that unless we first make you aware of something else." Then I was reminded of a question that I had put to my Church group just weeks before and it went like this:

How many of you believe Jesus will come during your lifetime?

To my great surprise, not a single person believed He would. I was deeply disappointed. Now the Father was similarly challenging me; albeit more personally. The coming of His Son was only one part of the equation—would we be ready for it—was the more important one, for whether He comes in our lifetime, we must (or should) be prepared to "meet our maker" at any moment, for any of us could die in an accident or health challenge.

I spent the next two weeks pondering this question. Finally, I had to conclude that "No," I was not ready if He were to come tomorrow. In the big scheme of things, I believed Jesus would return, but in my contemporary endeavors I was very much focused on other things like most newlyweds are: spouse, children, schooling, possibly a new location, job, a new church, the upkeep of motorcycles and cars, interests like gardening, other hobbies, etc., Taken as a whole, my life, as it was going, was consumed with the things of the world (granted, many were essentials).

It was on another prayer hike when I came to this realization, and my heart sank. I had been found spiritually wanting; I had become spiritually undone, and my spiritual countenance had fallen before God. Collapsing to my knees on that hill, I wept bitterly before God, and that is when it came, the thundering voice of God, and He said:

I am calling you unto Myself; forsake all else.

There I lay on that hill, prostrate, afraid, and amazed; it was a lot to take in—the voice of God, the message, and what it meant.

"Temple Hill" at The Ranch in Orinda CA; Wife and Son Pictured, 1994

This was God officially calling me into the wilderness. Our Lord came alongside me, consoled me, then said:

> You are to resign your pastorship and stop church life; you are no longer required to read the scriptures (searching them was allowed).

God wanted me to come to know Him like many of the prophets of old did who had neither church nor scriptures at their fingertips. So I resigned my pastorship, discontinued my psychology degree, resigned from my job, and we moved to a new area. Life for us changed significantly; I was in "that wilderness" for eight years; and there were other wildernesses after that.

Typically, what would occur, I would wake up to a full-blown vision of the place God wanted me to go that day to be taught. Once I arrived there, I would see a pillar of glory over the location, and then the teaching would begin. I would usually drive for an hour, and often hike for an additional hour or more; it would all depend on the location and what was going to be taught.

This is how my life was for the duration of that time, with my wife supporting me and sharing in each teaching that I would relate upon my return home.

PHOTO EXAMPLES

Trail Up

I would like to share some places where I was called to go. Many of these I had not visited for years until I went back to take pictures, and I was amazed to see a residue of God's glory still there. This is just a small sampling of the hundreds of spots I have been.

You will notice in many of the pictures a single tree. That's where the glory would come to and lighten the area. The following tree is atop a large mountain where I spent many hours communing with God and writing all that was revealed.

At a Single Tree Atop a Mountain

It was atop the following mountain where Jesus (and others) showed me I was doing what prophets of old had done going on prayer hikes to the tops of mountains, sometimes overlooking cities—to be taught from on High or to pray for those below:

23 And when he had sent the multitudes away, **he went up into a mountain apart to pray**: and when the evening was come, he was there alone. (Matthew 14)

12 And it came to pass in those days, that **he went out into a mountain to pray, and continued all night in prayer** to God. (Luke 6)

Where I Went to Commune With God

The following picture shows my view from the top of the previous mountain.

Prophet's View

Slightly above the center of the following picture is a single bench at a local park where I sat and communed with God for hours, and where He bathed *the entire area* with His wonder and presence.

Bench at Park

The following picture is of a picnic table under a group of pine trees.

Picnic Table Beneath Canopy of Trees

The following picture is of another picnic table beneath a canopy of trees.

Picnic Tables Beneath Canopy of Trees

The following picture is from the early 1990s, discerning God's glory.

Arlin Discerning God's Glory, Early 1990s

Bench Next to a Tree by a Lake

At a Table Next to a Sycamore

At a Picnic Table Next to a Pine Tree

Under a Bush Canopy Atop a Mountain

Amidst an Olive Orchard Atop a Mountain

I literally have thousands of pictures of my prayer hikes and teaching locations. After cell phones with cameras came out, it was easier to capture them in *real time*.

CHAPTER 7.

TESTIMONY OF GOD THE FATHER

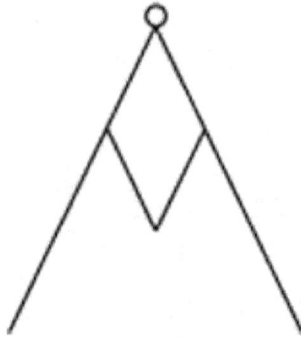

ALMIGHTY SYMBOL®

The Almighty symbol is a registered trademark which I designed in the glory of God the Father and is composed of the letters A-L-M-I-G-H-T-Y for those who can locate them.

The symbol represents a tall mountain where God the Father sits on a throne. God's throne is *very high* and is surrounded by clouds of glory that are continuously in motion. The downward lines extend outward while pointing downward and represent His extended arms that are ever reaching to us. The smaller upward lines represent the arms of those who are reaching up to Him.

God is like a KING
Who sits upon a THRONE
And is ALL POWERFUL
But, He is LIKE US

THE GLORY OF IT ALL

May 20, 2002

I have come to a well-known place that I have been many times before while writing the words of Saul and others. My prayer today and this entire week has been to know "How to distinguish between God the Father and the Son"? And this morning, God Our Father said He would answer my prayer.

As I sit parked in my vehicle surrounded by large oak trees, the glory of Our Father descends upon me. Some of the first distinguishing features I notice are: God is not on any assignment. He has nothing worldly from which I can reference Him. He is *perfect* and *whole*, completely round with no sharp edges from where He is from (historical point of origin), or to where He is going—there is no mantle of a mission He is on—He just IS.

He is ALL powerful, ALL wonderful, and there is no occasion to stumble when you see Him (expounded further down). There is no element regarding His nature that I can grasp. He just IS, and His ESSENCE is literally EVERYWHERE. We just don't know it because we have never been without it. Even to the leaves on a bush, He is there.

No matter how remote of an area, or how seemingly alone a plant or animal appear to be, God is there, and they are *content* and at *peace*. All of creation knows its place in space and time, for they are always in the company of Our Father. A star, a planet, they are all at peace, and never alone, for His presence is always there. He is with the light of the sun and the moon. He is with the light through which we move. He **accompanies** all of creation, and because of this, He cannot be discerned.

He is neither above it all, nor below it all. He IS—THE ALL. To all that is, and all that was, and all that will be—He is there.

The only way to know Him is if He turns His attention directly toward you. Then, it will seem as if all of creation, and all of time, are simultaneously focused just on YOU. You will then recognize the bounty of His presence near you. Then, you will acknowledge that His Essence exists all around you, and there is no place that exists that He is not.

There is no time that is, that He is not. Only in that moment will you realize that His Essence has a source, and that source has no beginning and no ending. It just **IS**. It is as we are AND all that is.

After experiencing this incredible introduction directly from Our Father, He then taught me how a person can discern Him. This is what He said:

> It is only by an increase in *amplitude* that the glory of my presence may be discerned.

Amplitude is "the amount by which a voltage or current changes" (*The American Heritage® Science Dictionary*).

For God is everywhere and in all things. We cannot exist without His presence. We can only *perceive a difference*. Not a difference in quality, for though white light may be split into the colors of a rainbow, its quality is never diminished—it is still "light" in a manner of speaking.

God Our Father may not be known by the manifold characteristics of His light, for He is present whenever His light is present, and there is no existence where His light is not present. Only a *magnification* of His light *from Him* can reveal its *true source*. Through such a magnification, can finally be seen a contrast from all that is. It is still the same light with no distinguishing properties.

The only difference is the MAGNITUDE, which is brought about by God's FOCUSED ATTENTION and that magnification will reveal its DIRECTION and SOURCE, which is God Our Father who is a DISTINCT BEING. I thank God Our Father for showing me an increase in His glory this day, and for the wonder and majesty it contained—the wonder of all time and all space being as a UNIFIED WHOLE; to a mortal, it was awesome to behold.

I would like to thank Our Father for always being mindful of His children, and for graciously answering my prayers.

SYMBOL OF OUR FATHER

As the teaching was ending, I glanced up at the Father and saw Him sitting on a throne looking down at me. I knew for that brief moment I was the most fortunate being in all of creation just to have His personal glance. I then drew the **Symbol of The Father**. It is like a calling card that can be used for contacting God. A person must be in the Spirit to feel and to see what the symbol means, but I shall describe it the best that I can.

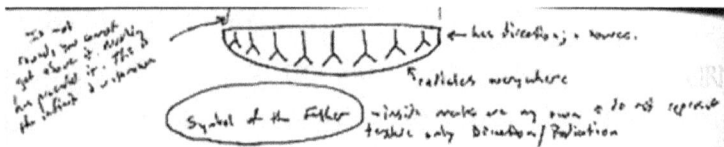

This is What I Drew in My Journal

As I looked into the glory of God The Father, I discovered several unique characteristics that I have not found with any other Heavenly Being.

First, Our Father's glory radiates everywhere. Imagine if you will a dome light cover that you find over a ceiling light. Imagine something that is fairly wide and slightly oval. Our Father's glory radiates like that; *except that it is as wide as eternity.* This is because His light is extending **EVERYWHERE.**

Second, Our Father's glory has a *source* and *direction.* The source is Him, and it is *constantly radiating outward* towards all creation, which gives it *direction.* These are the lines you see inside the dome. They do not represent texture, only **DIRECTION** and **RADI-ANCE**.

Third, the edge of the dome extends straight up for a while; this is because it is impossible for anyone to circumvent God The Father, physically, spiritually, energetically, conceptually, experientially, or any other way conceived.

RIPPLE EFFECT

I then wrote these words about the love God has for all of His children:

> As each child is different, Our Father is eager to see what they will manifest—a ripple effect throughout all creation.

Some ripples will go far, some will be catalysts for others, and some will cancel other ripples. It is an incredible dynamic that only Our Father can comprehend in its total expanse. Our lives have a purpose that goes far beyond anything we presently understand. As Our Father looks down upon us, I noticed He expresses these three attitudes:

- **God is eager for each child to live.**

- **God is curious to see what they will do.**

- **God is not afraid to give people a chance.**

These three attitudes helped me to understand *free will.* It's true; we DO ALL HAVE FREE WILL, therefore Our Father watches each of us with extreme interest **rather than acting like the future is already written in stone**. The show is **not** over.

Our Father clearly expressed to me that we DO have the power to do NEW THINGS. We are bound to neither the past nor the future. We who are alive have God and all of Heaven at our disposal—to do **something new**; He is waiting for someone to have the desire or courage to do so. This dynamic is happening all the time in the field of technology, for example, and Our Father glories in each new invention.

I have also wondered what God thinks of His creation overall. A fair percentage of His children appear to be turning away from what is good and praiseworthy. **Now I had the answer**. God is utterly **confident** and **optimistic,** and there is no occasion for stumbling in Him. We must respect His greater view, and that greater view is **joy, confidence,** and **optimism.**

God has given the gift of *self-awareness* to all of His children, which provides us with the ability to do many things. Most of Our Father's creations are run by His children with Jesus at the helm.

GOD IS TRUE AND FAITHFUL

I believe God is **true** and **faithful.** But let me put this in modern terms.

True means He is **fair.** His Word and their promises apply to every person of all ages.

Faithful means He is **willing**, as I described above, to give anyone a chance to perform something new.

Our God is fair, and Our God is willing.

Our Father, like any good father, is not respecting of His children. With each new child, He is anxious to see how they will learn and grow—to see what they will do and become; nothing is set in stone. If they are eager, then it is His job to keep that fire burning and well fed.

ONE WEEK LATER

It has been one week after God Our Father revealed Himself and taught me, and the residue of His almighty power and glory is still with me, so I sat down to write theses additional words.

Holy Father: Holy means complete, perfectly sound.

1. Why is this wonderful? Because He is the only one that is like this. It is what we are not, just by virtue of the fact He has always existed and we have not. We have a beginning. He doesn't.

2. We have a point of origin, and that is like a jagged edge to our spiritual character. He doesn't have any jagged edges in His character.

3. With each jagged edge, we cast a shadow—it's what shapes who we are. Our Father has no shadows.

4. He is the ultimate source of spiritual light. There is no other light that shines above Him; therefore, there can never be a shadow cast upon Him.

5. Every person has a spiritual shadow.

6. Our Father's light has a *quality* that we can rightly call *love* (thank goodness). It feels good, and it is comforting, and peaceful. It is harmonious and coherent. His love has qualities of GREAT INTEREST, GREAT EXPECTATION, and GREAT BELIEF.

7. It is so wonderful and I joy in writing about God.

8. All things were made with love.

9. All things are happy to exist, for they are all comforted by His endless love.

10. "Endless," because it literally has *no beginning* and *no end.*

11. He is so JOYFUL. The joy of Our Father is to bring forth the eternal life of His children.

12. He has only *positive, joyful expectations* for all of us.

13. Like a mechanic who is proud of his car's performance, so too is Our Father proud of

the doings of His children.

14. He smiles as He looks down upon His children, and it is as wide as the universe—*God is literally smiling.*

15. You can feel God and His love in your bosom, and God can feel you in His heart, and He knows how we each are doing.

16. Even a single blade of grass is **KNOWN** and, therefore, **NOT ALONE.**

We hear of this ability of God the Father often—that He knows every sparrow that falls—Jesus talked about it. I want to testify to the truth of this. This is *an ability* that God has; He can perceive all of creation at the same time. This is not an expression, it is an **ABILITY.** Of this, I testify.

In my treatise called *Set God Free* (chapter is included further down) I share the one question anyone can ask the Father and get His personal attention and INTERVENTION. And that was given to me by revelation from the highest authority there is. Until then, let me share one last thing that the Father directed me to.

After I finished this writing, Our Father instructed me to walk to a distant wall; I did not know why. As I approached the wall, I discovered it had a plaque on the other side. I took a picture of this plaque, it's "The Lord's Prayer." I stood in awe as I realized this is not "The Lord's" prayer, but it's "God the Father's" prayer as given to us **through** Jesus.

Plaque of The Lord's Prayer – to The Father

OUR FATHER who art in Heaven
Hallowed be **THY NAME**
THY KINGDOM come
THY WILL be done
On earth as it is in Heaven
Give us this day our daily bread
Forgive us our debts as we forgive our debtors
Lead us not into temptation but deliver us from evil
For
THINE IS THE KINGDOM
and
THE GLORY FOR EVER
Amen

When we recite this prayer, who are we thinking of: Jesus or God the Father? My heart ached as I realized this has not been understood by His children. I testify that this prayer is for **Our Father** and it is all about **Him,** and **His Kingdom**.

WHY PEOPLE FALL DOWN & PRAISE?

Upon entering into the presence of Our Father or His Son, or a holy messenger, the first response from the receiver is: "Why has God favored me with such greatness?" Why this response? Because immortal beings are far superior to us mortals, and their mere presence can *overwhelm* us.

Receivers of the divine presence are not just awestruck, like those who stand in wonder of a meteor shower. No. They fall to the ground, flat on their faces, and start sounding *anthems of praise*. Why do they do this? Because the magnificence of the power they are beholding is enveloped in LOVE, not fear.

The question they then seek to understand is: "Why is it that such an incredible, all-powerful, immortal being as this could have such love for a mortal sinner as I?" For God and Heavenly messengers to have such respect and acknowledgment for one so inferior speaks volumes about their *eternal kindness* that it spurs a response of *gratitude* from the receiver so great that they are unable to do so sufficiently, and thus become *overwhelmed*.

We can never give thanks or praise enough to THE ONE who has existed for ALL ETERNITY, who is without beginning of days or end of years. Try as we might, we will become *overwhelmed*.

CHAPTER 8.

RETURN TO THE FATHER

---

*Grace be to you and peace from **God the Father**,*
and from our Lord Jesus Christ. (Galatians 1:3)

Jesus came into the world out of obedience to Our Heavenly Father. And He gave us the words of life out of obedience to Our Heavenly Father. He showed us by His actions how we should live before Our Heavenly Father. He taught us how to pray to Our Heavenly Father. Jesus died so that we may return to Our Heavenly Father. Jesus is the propitiation for our sins before Our Heavenly Father. He did all things for Our Heavenly Father.

However, all of our churches are named after Jesus. Most of our songs, sermons, and writings are about Jesus. Did God Our Father create a being more powerful than Himself? What has happened to Our Heavenly Father? If we have built upon the foundation set by Jesus, we should have large numbers of churches, books, songs, and books about Our Heavenly Father. Why is this not the case? How important is Our Heavenly Father to Jesus? These and many other questions I have received answers to, and I am commissioned by Almighty God to share them.

Let me first testify that I know God lives, for I have seen Him. I have seen His face, and I have seen His glory, and I know He lives. Just as Stephen saw the Heavens opened and saw God sitting upon His throne and Jesus standing on His right hand, so too, have the Heavens opened to me and I have seen Him. He revealed Himself to me.

God Our Father lives! And the testimonies about Him are true. He IS our Father, and He resides in our home, the home from which we all have come, and the place He desires all of His children to return.

You may test my words to see if they are not true, for though many clever men have configured mighty "truths," it is nothing but the pure knowledge from Almighty God that reveals their origins. And the test of all prophets is whether they have conveyed any new truth. Today, I will again share new truths as they have been given to me by Him, and they are given to serve His purpose and not my own.

Do not waste your time with the theories of men, for unless they can testify that they have been taught from on High, they are only perpetuating the theories and ideologies of man, and confusing God's children. **God is not the author of confusion** and does not wish for His children to be disillusioned.

I testify God is real and the day of man's reckoning is coming. All men will be accountable for the teachings they have shared, whether they are of God or man. We have the freedom to explore the creations of our own mind, **but we do not have the freedom to push those upon others as if they are the truth.**

God Our Father is coming, and nobody in the world knows it. They know Jesus is coming, and they have been focusing their attention on that, but they do not know about God the Father. I testify that the entire world is under sin, and they need to turn to God their Father. And unless they do so, they may be met with the chastening hand of Almighty God—that they might learn that He IS a **jealous God**.

Behold what the Holy Word of God Our Father says:

> 27 For the Son of man shall come **in the glory of HIS FATHER** with **HIS angels [i.e., God Our Father's angels!]**; and then he shall reward every man according to his works. (Matthew 16)

Jesus proclaimed this while on the earth, saying, though you have confessed my name, or have been baptized as I—it is not enough unless you know God the Father, and do His will:

> 21 Not **every one that saith unto me, Lord, Lord**, shall enter into the kingdom of heaven; but he that doeth the **will of MY FATHER** which is in heaven. (Matthew 7; confessing Jesus is not enough for even the devils confess)

> 23 Ye shall drink indeed of my cup **and be**

baptized with the baptism that I am baptized with: but to sit on my right hand, and on my left, is not mine to give, but it shall be given to them for whom it is **prepared of MY FATHER.** (Matthew 20; baptism is not enough)

Let's read how Jesus wanted us to view Him and God the Father:

17 And he said unto him, **Why callest thou me good?** *there is* none good but one, *that is,* **God.** (Matthew 19)

24 Verily, verily, I say unto you, He that heareth my word, and **BELIEVETH ON HIM that sent me,** hath everlasting life, and **shall not come into condemnation**; but is passed from death unto life. (John 5)

44 No man can come to me, **EXCEPT THE FATHER which hath sent me draw him**: and I will raise him up at the last day. (John 6)

16 Jesus answered them, and said, **My doctrine IS NOT MINE,** but his that sent me.
17 **If any man will do his will, he shall know of the doctrine, WHETHER IT BE OF GOD,** or whether I speak of myself. (John 7)

44 Jesus cried and said, He that believeth on me, **BELIEVETH NOT ON ME, BUT ON HIM THAT SENT ME.** (John 12)

49 For **I have not spoken of myself; BUT THE FATHER which sent me, HE GAVE ME A COMMANDMENT**, what I should say, and what I should speak. (John 12)

6 But thou, when thou prayest, enter into thy closet, and when thou hast shut thy door, **PRAY TO THY FATHER** which is in secret. (Matthew 6)

As God Our Father looks down upon us, His children, He sees a lot of misdirection and a lot of misunderstanding. How is it that so many people are reading these words about Him but are not focusing their attention on Him?

8 Philip saith unto him, Lord, **shew us the Father**, and it sufficeth us.
9 Jesus saith unto him, Have I been so long time with you, and yet hast thou not known me, Philip? **he that hath seen me hath seen the Father**; and how sayest thou *then*, Shew us the Father? (John 14)

Even His own people, with all of their history and testimony, would not accept Jesus, and so they killed him. Today, there remain many with that same belief system, despite the millions of Christians that say otherwise. And now, His followers are under a veil of misdirection as to who the **one true God** is.

29 And Jesus answered him, **The first of all the commandments *is***, Hear, O Israel; **The Lord**

our God is one Lord:
30 And **thou shalt love the Lord thy God with all thy heart**, and with all thy soul, and with all thy mind, and with all thy strength: **this *is* the first commandment**. (Mark 12)

The misdirection is troubling, for it will detour His followers from returning home to The Father. What I will share next is a vision of the future, exactly how God Our Father showed me. It involves millions of Christians who have been misdirected.

VISION OF THE MILLENNIUM

As it stands, millions of Christians are waiting for the Second Coming of the Lord Jesus Christ when He will reign over the earth for a thousand years in peace, or what is commonly called "The Millennium." At the return of Jesus Christ, everyone will have the testimony that Jesus is the Son of God. Once that has been established, i.e., when it becomes common knowledge that Jesus is Lord, his Sonship will never need to be proclaimed again.

Consider all the Christian churches. They are all over the world, in almost every nation, proclaiming Christ. What happens when first-hand knowledge replaces that, and it no longer needs to be taught? Right now it is Christ who Christians live for, pray for, and hope to see coming. What will they live for after Jesus arrives?

The previous longing and hoping will be gone, so

what is left? This is what I saw in Spirit, and what I will share now.

If Jesus were all there was, then our eternal life would be sealed the moment He appeared. But I did not see that. What I saw taking place was continual learning, but what was being taught? They were learning the things Jesus already instructed two thousand years ago—the same things that have been taught in Sunday School everywhere, but not understood.

There was one difference—Jesus was not the focus—for He already arrived. But the reason they were studying His words *all over again* was to read them in their proper context. What they had previously learned was centered on Jesus, but He never said to do that. Jesus explicitly stated that He was only [not to make light of it] "the way" and not "the destination." He is a Son; He is not the Father—ponder that difference. Jesus was a messenger, *not the sender* of the message.

The reason they were reading Jesus' words all over again was to see them in their correct frame of reference. No person could ever expect to get to The Father if they did not have an accurate understanding of Him. I saw that Christians knew all about Jesus when He arrived, but virtually nothing about God the Father, which makes His messenger Jesus look as if He failed in His assignment of pointing people to God the Father.

Jesus is not here to glorify Himself, but to glorify God Our Father. He does not want us to pray to Him (though He tolerates it), worship Him (though He allows it), or to focus solely on Him. If we want His respect, then we will do what He said by putting our attention on God the Father. Once again, He is asking that we **do the will of The Father**:

50 For whosoever shall do the **WILL OF MY FATHER which is in heaven, the same is MY BROTHER**, and sister, and mother. (Matthew 12)

Jesus would never take glory unto Himself. He proved that when He died on the cross. And He doesn't want to take attention away from God Our Father. It is the inability to move on to **spiritual independence** with God that is keeping most Christians focused on Jesus. Jesus is undoubtedly worthy to learn from, but not to focus *all* of our attention.

Paul knew this well. During his time, he, like Jesus, saw the inclination of people to marvel at the power of Jesus' name, and to focus their attention solely upon Him. Though Jesus is worthy, He is not Our Father. The way we honor Jesus is by showing our understanding of what He taught and then moving towards perfection like God the Father is perfect:

48 **Be ye therefore PERFECT, even as YOUR FATHER which is in HEAVEN is PERFECT**. (Matthew 5)

1 Therefore **LEAVING the principles of the DOCTRINE OF CHRIST**, let us go on unto

perfection **not laying again the foundation** of repentance from dead works, and of faith toward God,

2 Of the doctrine of baptisms, and of laying on of hands, and of resurrections of the dead, and of eternal judgment. (Hebrews 6)

The only people who would draw offense to those words by the apostle Paul are those who have not yet come to know God the Father—the Father of Our Lord Jesus. If we as Christians are fascinated with the Lordship of Jesus, why don't we desire to learn about **His Father?**

9 Furthermore we have had fathers of our flesh which corrected *us,* and we gave *them* reverence: **shall we not MUCH RATHER be in SUBJEC-TION unto the FATHER OF SPIRITS, and live?** (Hebrews 12)

Jesus has clearly stated the importance of this, but it is continually overlooked. Take, for example, the *Parable of the Wise Man* that built his house upon a rock. What is that parable talking about? If we review it in the light of this revelation, we learn that Jesus was talking about those who don't do the will of God Our Father.

This parable follows on the heels of the passage I cited earlier, where Jesus explained how confessing his name would not be enough to get us into the Kingdom of Heaven; only doing the **will of God Our**

Father will do that. With this point of reference in mind, let us review those scriptures next:

> 21 Not **every one that saith unto me, Lord, Lord,** shall enter into the kingdom of heaven; but he that doeth the **will of my Father** which is in heaven. (Matthew 7)

We see the parable is a warning to those who build their life and their faith *only* upon Jesus and not on God Our Father. Now couple that verse with the following warning:

> 24 Therefore whosoever heareth these sayings of mine, and doeth them, I will liken him unto a wise man, **which built his house upon a rock: 26 And every one that heareth these sayings of mine, and doeth them not...great was the fall of it.** (Matthew 7)

It could be a fantastic house for a while, like so many churches and ministries are, but unless we know Our Father, we won't be drawing our strength from our ultimate source. Jesus warned:

> 13 **Every plant, which MY HEAVENLY FATHER hath not planted, shall be ROOTED UP.** (Matthew 15)

Jesus did everything that He could to teach the people about God The Father. He said He came from Our Father, said He was going to Our Father and stated He was only teaching the doctrine that Our Father gave to Him, etc.

> 25 **O righteous Father, the world hath NOT KNOWN THEE**: but I have known thee, and these have known that thou hast sent me.
> 26 And **I have declared unto them thy name**, and will declare it: (John 17)

If only it could be on our lips, like it was on the apostle Paul's:

> 6 That ye may with one mind and one mouth **glorify God, EVEN THE FATHER of our Lord Jesus Christ**. (Romans 15)

We have other reasons why we would do well to keep our focus upon God the Father. For one, the angels report to Our Father:

> 4 And the smoke of the incense, *which came* with the **prayers** of the saints, **ascended up before God out of the angel's hand**. (Revelation 8)

> 10 That in heaven their **angels** do always behold the **face of MY FATHER** which is in heaven. (Matthew 18)

A second reason to keep our focus upon God Our Father is because He is the only one who knows when the world will end. If we are to be ready for that event, then He is the one we should keep our focus upon:

36 But of that day and hour knoweth no man, no, not the angles of heaven, **but MY FATHER only**. (Matthew 24)

Third, what will separate the 144,000 from all the other people is not just that they are virgins, but that they are doing the will of "The Father" and they will receive the stamp of Our Father's name in their foreheads:

1 An hundred forty and four thousand, having **his FATHER'S NAME written in their foreheads**. (Revelation 14)

The Rock of Revelation and the will of God Our Father will guide all who seek Him. Those of us who walk in His Spirit will never be satisfied until we are back in His presence, and in His holy arms: **God is Our Father, and we ARE His children**.

CONCLUSION

I testify that the reason we are living is to prove a preference for God and His love. Not Jesus (solely), not self-love, not brotherly love, not the love of the flesh, nor the opposite sex, but of Father God. That is the only thing. Jesus, as our exemplar, made that clear. He never assumed what would be pleasing to Our Father. He always first found out what Our Father's will was, and then He did that.

What is pleasing to Our Father is to know His will for our life, and then to do it. God is real, He is alive, and He can hear us. God has also written His will upon our hearts if we will but respect our conscience. Only the individual will know whether they are fulfilling Their Father's will for their life or not:

> 33 After those days, saith the LORD, I will put my law in their inward parts, and **write it in their hearts**; and will be their God, and they shall be my people.
> 34 And **they shall teach no more every man his neighbour**, and every man his brother, saying, Know the LORD: **for they shall all know me**, from the least of them unto the greatest of them, saith the LORD; (Jeremiah 31)

I testify that God loves all of us, His children, and He will continue to fulfill our different needs through His many legions of angels and others. But we are not here to give the angels something to do. We are here to prove above all else that **God Our Father IS our preference**, and He is worthy of all of our attention. Then, and only then, will The Father say:

My son/daughter, you have proven yourself worthy to inherit all that I have, enter in ye blessed of the Lord. (Matthew 25:23)

CHAPTER 9.

GOD THE FATHER'S LOVE

What happened early in the year of 1998 changed my perspective, and my life, forever.

FIVE BRIGHT STARS

Back in 1997-98, in less than six months, five very prominent people suddenly died. Those deaths caught my attention. I asked God the Father if there was a message here. He answered that there was. He did not respond through the subtle whisperings of the Spirit; instead, He replied to me in a cloud of glory. The glory was so thick, so real, that its presence significantly changed me.

Then Our Father taught me in a way only He could, and that was *conceptually* through His greater wisdom. After I understood Our Father's view, it changed my perspective, allowing me to see things in a new way. No longer would I *theorize* that God loves all of His children. I learned it firsthand.

Of the five very prominent people suddenly taken, the first was **Princess Diana**, she died *August 31, 1997.* The second was **Mother Teresa**; she died *Sep-*

tember 05, 1997. The third was **John Denver**; he died *October 12, 1997*. The fourth was **Michael Kennedy**; he died *December 31, 1997*. And the fifth person was **Sonny Bono**, who died on *January 05, 1998*.

PICTURES

Princess Diana (d. August 31, 1997)

Mother Teresa (d. September 05, 1997)

John Denver (d. October 12, 1997)

Michael Kennedy (d. December 31, 1997)

Sonny Bono (d. January 05, 1998)

EXPLANATION

Our Father told me that indeed these very public figures were taken because they were "the best the Earth had." These were five of our brightest lights. "But," I asked, "Princess Diana was drinking and having relations with men; John Denver was caught driving under the influence; Michael Kennedy had relations with a babysitter; and Sonny Bono was married four times."

Our kind Father replied:

From your view, that is all you see. From My view, I only see glory.

"Glory about what?" I replied. Then Our Father taught me why He only looks on the inside of a person, and not the outside. Only God knows the circumstances that a person is born into. Only He knows who has increased their station in life, and who has wasted their time.

Each one of these individuals had obtained some degree of fame. It could have been very easy for any of them to bask in the light of their popularity and not care about those around them. But they did not. Each person, I found out, had indeed sought different ways to raise the plight of humanity. They did so out of their *own free will*, even at significant risk and sacrifice.

1. Princess Diana was a "People's Princess." That is why everyone loved her so much. Diana braved the waters where others dare not go. When no one else would, she showed compassion for those with AIDS. She had compassion for those who lost their legs from war mines that were never removed. She had tenderness for people everywhere she went. It would have been easy for her to enjoy being in the limelight of the adoring public and of the palace, but she never felt comfortable in doing so.

Princess Diana and Mother Teresa were friends. Both were true Saints. The world honored Princess Diana after her tragic death by doing what she loved to do—*donate money.* The *Diana, Princess of Wales Memorial Fund,* was set up and quickly grew to over 56 million dollars; her legacy continues to this day.

2. Mother Teresa. Most people know about Mother Teresa, but did we know she was sincere? Mother Teresa was not in Calcutta out of duty, she was there out of love, and she served those people faithfully all of her life. She was a Saint in every sense of the word. She received the Nobel Prize *for Peace* in 1979. Mother Teresa is the one who said: "It's not how much you do, but how much love you put into it." Her legacy also continues.

3. John Denver blessed the world with music that was joyful and uplifting. The causes that John supported include *The National Wildlife Federation, Save The Children, The Hunger Project, The Cousteau Society, The Windstar Foundation, Friends of the Earth, Plant-it 2002,* and the *Human/Dolphin Foundation.* Until the end, John Denver fought for environmental causes. Our Father respected this, more than John Denver's moment(s) of drunkenness. Overall, John Denver made God proud, and his legacy also goes on.

4. Michael Kennedy is not as well known, but the Kennedy family is. Michael stood out from others because he cared about the elderly and the poor. He headed *Citizens Energy Corp.*, a nonprofit organization:

> Under Michael Kennedy's leadership, Citizens launched humanitarian relief missions to Eastern Europe, Angola, Congo, Namibia, and Nigeria while expanding Citizens' charitable programs on the African continent, including efforts to remove deadly landmines from the Angolan landscape. He also helped launch an award-winning initiative to stop handgun violence and created a new charitable venture supporting programs and research to benefit the homeless, the uninsured, and others without access to quality health care. (Company website)

He is the one who said: "One person can make a difference in this world if they really try." His work and legacy also endures.

5. Sonny Bono blessed the world with his cheerfulness, his music, and his humor. I had the good fortune of seeing him and Cher perform at Six Flags Magic Mountain early in their career. Sonny ran for public office and was elected mayor of Palm Springs, and then Congressman (twice). He served all the days of his life, fighting for valiant causes.

Other Congressmen said of Sonny Bono that he

was a "people's politician." He would dress in *blue jeans*, and was as down to earth as any person could be. His second wife Mary has carried forward the work he started, and she has been re-elected three times.

SUMMATION

These five very prominent people were not without faults, but God took them because He said: "They were the best the world had." It doesn't matter what others say about these five people, or whom they say God accepts. I care about what Our Father personally explained to me. I know He is using them for His own purposes on the other side. I have never forgotten that teaching from Our Father, and I never will.

If I should be so fortunate to have Our Father look upon me as favorably as He did upon them, that is all I would ever desire. These five deserve a greater tribute than I have given, and blessed be the person who does it. From that day until now, Our Father has continued to help me learn how **He** views His children. My mindset is now broader, and I am a better person for it.

I testify God took these five, and I testify that God taught me from on high regarding what He respects in a person's life, and what He doesn't. I testify that the entire world, both the dead and the living, can learn this lesson as well. The next teaching Our Father gave on this topic came about two years later.

THE CHINESE MAN

I was on my way to work as usual one morning. I sat on the bus watching people get on and off at each stop. It was mostly quiet in the mornings, which provided an excellent time to be taught from on High, and that is what Our Father did. In an instant, I was being taught about who we are as humanity.

I looked around, and I saw people of all nationalities and faiths. In particular, I was looking at a short, old Chinese man sitting right across from me. He looked about as foreign as a person could look. As I was looking at this man, Our Father began to teach me.

He showed me how this man (who had a body type different from my own and spoke a different language) was in reality *just along for the ride on earth.* In fact, before he even entered that mortal body, we were the same. Do we realize that each nationality was not set in heaven and that we don't currently look how we did before coming to earth? The realization of that was far-reaching for me; it was a life-changing moment. **I could have just as easily entered his body as he could have entered mine.**

As spirits, we were the same—children of God. For one moment, I could see and realize that we were all just *along for the ride.* So much is dictated throughout our life by the external environment, e.g., our upbringing, people who influence us, and most importantly—our DNA. Once the externals are accounted for, we can see that we are all "just along for the ride."

Certainly, there are choices which can further define us, but we should not be so quick to judge others based just on what we see. Each of us is fully aware of the ride we are going to experience upon entering the human family. Some "life packages" are so set in stone that to go into that life package would take more courage than to go into a life package the exact opposite. This understanding is part of God's view that only He has. It is far above what we mortals can comprehend.

WHEN WE DREAM

To support the teaching that we are all along for the ride, I would like to share what I know about our dream state. It is something we all do as human beings. There is nobody on this earth who does not dream. Or, another way to put it, everybody has the opportunity to evaluate their life package on a daily basis and try to change it.

These dreams are hardly ever remembered, but perhaps everyone has had at least one from which they can learn. The dream would be of you observing yourself *objectively*, i.e., a third-person viewpoint. Perhaps in the dream you are visiting with others, and all of you are sharing in an *objective* discussion of each other's life package, and how difficult it is to bring change to the waking, rational mind.

I have had a few of these dreams. They were teaching dreams, and that is why I was permitted to remember them. In each case, the objectivity of my spirit toward my life package was remarkable. The spirit may try with all its might to give direction that the waking mind will follow, but this can be most difficult depending on the life package involved.

I have even seen the objectivity of serious offenders on earth, who did not wish to continue in their life package, and did not like to experience what their life package was doing. Though try as they might, the package was *so set* they were truly just along for the ride. We can rest assured that Our Father sees us only as His children, and not the life package we have.

Therefore, we should respect others who have entered life packages more challenging than our own, and admire their souls for having the courage to do so. Lastly, let us put our focus on the weightier matters like the *Five Bright Stars* did, and do those things that will bless humanity and be pleasing to God.

DAY OF THE ROBIN

[The following testimony comes from Spiritual Journeys – Vol. 3, and has since been retired.]

The following miracle, I was instructed to call "Day of the Robin" and demonstrates the love of God well. This experience with the robins I never expected to share with anyone but my family. But I have been commanded to write about it. The date was *Sunday, December 23, 2001.*

I had been very sad as the holiday season replaced my work in glory with God the Father. I don't know what it is—the changing of seasons, the closing of another year, the commotion associated with the holidays, but I often feel a profound sense of melancholy, so I went for a walk to one of my favorite locations. The sky was dotted with billowy clouds; no one was on the trail where I entered, and I headed north.

I did not walk long before the glory of God fell upon the area. I was fascinated by the trees that were around me. They did not have leaves, and yet they were still able to interact with the glory that descended upon them. Usually, I see the glory as the green leaves capture it and they become illuminated by God's Light. What I was now seeing was new to me, so I just stopped and watched what was before and around me. God's Light not only touched me but also the *limbs* of the trees.

Soon, the entire area became saturated with God's presence. It was so thick I could take but one step and then I would have to pause and PRAISE God and THANK Him for His poured-out LOVE. Suddenly, I heard a loud noise ahead, around the next bend, like birds in the distance. I continued my walk north, just one step at a time, all the while basking in the tremendous Light of His Presence while my aching soul was simultaneously being restored.

As I went northward, the sound of birds grew

louder and *louder*. I shifted my attention away from the path I was on and looked to my left at the source of this *great cacophony*, and I could not believe my eyes. There, in the tops of several gigantic oaks, I saw hundreds, no, thousands of birds. They seemed like birds of all types and sizes moving about with great excitement.

I moved closer so I could fully appreciate the scene before me. As I did so, I could distinguish what kind of bird they were, and to my awestruck surprise, I saw row upon row, branch upon branch, filled with **ROBINS**. I stood in utter amazement. My heart swelled even more with profound joy. My mind was connected to a time back in my childhood when I was innocent and had a profound love for robins, and then I realized it had connected me to God.

Without exaggeration, every upper branch and limb in these large oak trees were lined with red Robins. They were not just sitting still, but were heartily interacting with one another. They stayed right there within the tops of the trees for the duration that I stood there; not a single robin flew away. It's hard to explain what it was like seeing such a vast quantity of birds all in one place.

The best way I can describe it is by what you commonly see at pet stores that sell birds—particularly Finches, when they are all lined up on one rod sitting side by side with no spaces between them. That is what I saw on every branch of the trees. The activity was so great and the noise so loud; it seemed as if the robins were multiplying right before my eyes. I then heard another loud roar of birds and great excitement across the creek, and to my surprise, I saw several giant eucalyptus trees that began swarming with robins, and yet I never saw a single robin fly to either of these trees. They were indeed multiplying before my very eyes.

I would say that the birds concentrated themselves on five trees—two eucalyptus and three oaks. This is a picture of those trees, taken at a later date:

Day of The Robin – Two Giant Oak Trees

Though I had been on this trail hundreds of times, I had never seen a single robin before nor since that day. I even waited an entire year before writing this so that I could visit the exact spot at the same time to find one, but none were there. God alone deserves the credit for the miracle that He performed for me that day, and I humbly share this testimony for all to know.

I stand in awe at how God respected the tender memories I had as a little child. I marvel at His love for the simple pleasures of nature, and rejoice in His pleasure to bless others with it. There is a movie called *Dragon Fly*, and I have heard of similar stories where birds or insects have multiplied themselves or even followed a person to serve a *divine purpose*. As I write this, I am reminded of the time Our Lord multiplied the fishes in Peters net and the quail for the children of Israel.

Truly God is all-powerful and can multiply fully grown fish, birds, or animals in the blink of an eye. God has used birds at other times in my life to spur me on, and I know that others have had similar experiences as well. I don't look for signs, but sometimes God just wants to say, "I'm mindful of you" in a remarkable way. I would not encourage others to look for signs, but don't be surprised if God uses nature to bless your life in amazing situations.

I have now fulfilled the commandment to write of this experience and to document the love that God has for each of His children. From the day of that event until now, The Father has encouraged me to share it. Even now, as I write, The Father is very firm **that this miracle be shared**. Whether in Heaven or on earth, I know not, but I know it is of great worth before Him.

CHAPTER 10.

GOD THE FATHER'S VIEW OF ADULT CHILDREN

Holy Father, my heart aches and pains for Your will to come true among us, and I know I would not have these pains if Your love was not so real to me, and yet it is very real for You have revealed Yourself to me. I know that Your will for each of Your children is that they experience JOY, and if they are not experiencing it, then I know Your joy is not full.

Our Father has further revealed His view of humanity to me—not just as spirits or innocent children—but as adults. Because God is love, it has been impossible for me to ever conceive of a mean Father like the Old Testament sometimes shows. I, like others, have struggled to understand what this means, and today I have been given its understanding.

The following view is not altogether new, for I have seen it employed by others who work for God who are more qualified than I in their views of humanity. It goes like this:

1. They do know of the greatness of God and His amazing love, mercy, and grace.

2. They do also know of the incredible opportunities we have on earth.

3. But for them to see people wasting their time on earth, they have some disdain. Why? **Because, where much is given, much is expected.**

Have we been given much? Yes, we have. And if we purposely abuse it, then God's tolerance is lessened. Our Father has a *low tolerance* for those who are abusing or neglecting the opportunities given them. What we see in the Old Testament is a *low tolerance* for abusing the favor God gave.

If we only see God's wrath and not the misuse of what was given, then God's treatment may appear excessive. But if God is not extreme, then His treatment must be equal to the neglect that was displayed by one of His children. If any treatment seems excessive, it is because *He has given exceedingly much.*

We know how God feels about children—that they are innocent before Him; that they as yet have no judgments and no limits. Jesus pronounced "woes" against anyone that offends little ones, or in other words:

"Woe to him that judges and limits what God has given to His children!"

We have freedom *how* to fulfill what is given, but we do not have the right to mock that freedom by wasting it.

This concept was relayed in *The Parable of the Talents*, and it shows that before God, when a stewardship is given, the capacity to fulfill that stewardship is also given. If a stewardship was given without the capacity to fulfill it, then abuse and neglect by the individual could be warranted. But as children of God, our capacity is great, and we can overcome most things.

Part of that capacity is the element of spirit, and a person may not abuse or neglect their life regardless of their human abilities. The history of humanity is full of great accomplishments that defy all reason. To the first person who denied their capacity for greatness, God said:

> 6 And the Lord said unto Cain, Why art thou wroth? And why is thy countenance fallen?
> 7 **If thou doest well, shalt thou not be accepted? And if thou doest not well, sin lieth at the door.** And unto thee shall be his desire, and thou shalt rule over him. (Genesis 4)

"Sin" is when we separate ourselves from God. Another way people sin and separate themselves from God is by *not fulfilling the destiny that God has given them.* Our Father cannot look upon sin or separation from His will (which is to have **joy**) with the least degree of allowance.

He has birthed each of us with the ability to fulfill greatness *in our own way,* and if we have lost that ability, then we are good for nothing but to be trodden under the feet of people like salt that has lost its savour. If left unchecked, that sin would perpetuate itself for generations, and there would be no end to the extent people might abuse or neglect the abilities and opportunities given them.

For this reason, God will start fresh (like with Noah and Abraham) or obliterate the offenders (Sodom and Gomorrah). A father corrects children he loves, and the Old Testament is full of the chastening hand of God, and Our Father *will not hesitate* to send chastening again to those not doing His divine will, for where much is given, much is required. And that is the difference in views between innocent children and adult children.

Nusbaum Family, USA, 2019

CHAPTER 11.

SET GOD FREE

Recently there have been some disturbing events (trafficking of children) that have caused my heart to ache and to wonder. On the morning of July 17th, 2002, I poured out my heart to Our Father and said,

> How long Holy Father will thou stay Thy hand amid so much trouble?

In my heart, the question was actually:

What will it take to get you to intervene at this time?

I am sure we have all been pained by the injustices that seem to be continually before us. I think we could all agree that if ever a time in history needed God's intervention in a biblical way, it could be now.

On that same morning, at precisely seven o'clock, I received an answer from Father God, and I desire to share His response. It wasn't just a yes or no answer; it was a teaching of truths that I had not previously understood. As always, Our Father taught the principles, and the answer was self-revealing.

The first principle Our Father taught was about human suffering.

HUMAN SUFFERING

Our Father blessed me to understand how He views humanity. Because we are in the world, our physical condition is everything to us. Many of us judge our worthiness by how well things are physically in our life. Our Father, however, does not always bless us in that way; He looks at things differently.

Aside from the fact that God is above all of mortality, there are other reasons why His perspective is above our own. Knowing that His children are made of spirit, and the flesh is only our temporal abode, He is not *overly* concerned about our physical condition, as much as He is about our *spiritual* condition.

First, Our Father wanted me to understand that His concern is not with human suffering so much as it is with *spiritual apathy*. If we could only appreciate how long it took God to prepare this earthly environment, and how long it took Him to create these complex societies, then we could understand His concern for spiritual apathy over human suffering.

Each soul only gets one chance at this earth life. If that opportunity gets taken from them, they will have literally missed the "chance of a lifetime"—for *spiritual development*. It is the loss of growth, more than temporal suffering, that concerns Our Father the most.

Our Father said He is not concerned by the tragic deaths of these people, *for all die.* But He is quite concerned and *outright saddened* when a person's *right for growth and freedom to explore is taken.* He made this point absolutely clear, and I testify that *this is the case.* I'll repeat, how long did it take God to prepare this earth and its current environment of growth, learning, and experience? More than we can comprehend.

It would be analogous to creating a vast amusement park like Disney World and bringing many busloads of kids and tourists from the other side of the world, but then not letting them into the park to experience it. The next concept Our Father helped me to understand was the divine order of things.

DIVINE ORDER

Our Father answered the second part of my question, which had to do with *intervention.* He assured me that intervention could not come easily. In order for Our Father to assist all of creation, and our entire earthly family, He requires *a great deal of support.* To help Him in those efforts, Our Father has called and appointed *many* into positions of leadership, from His throne down to each person's guardian angel.

When Our Father did that, He granted them each some degree of autonomy, and He respects their decisions—for the most part. Our Father said that although He is God, it is against divine order for Him or anyone else to interfere in another's stewardship; if this were not so, there would be chaos. He completely respects the leadership of those to whom He has entrusted with those positions.

To me, this sounded logical, and in harmony with how I know Our Father works—God is not going to step in on your family. There *are* spiritual rulers who preside over "high places," i.e., their domain encompasses "a lot of territory" (everything comprises territories). Their task is to serve *transparently* with Our Father so as not to draw attention to themselves (it is forbidden to worship angels; Col.2:18).

Our focus, and all glory, should go to God the Father because He IS worthy—whether or not we realize it. Those rulers in high places are assigned over continents, nations, and peoples, and God respects their jurisdiction. This *concept* represented the confidence Our God has in His people. I testify that this is how God works, and that He respects the stewardship of those whom He has appointed.

Though change is often slow, God still respects their work. Others may prefer to believe in a God who works magically, and everything is mysteriously done, but that does not empower the individual for producing change. After I understood those two concepts—*human suffering* and *divine order*—Our Father then said:

All was not lost.

He said there is one prayer that we can pray that would bypass those rulers and authorize His direct intervention without breaking the order. He said He would teach me that next. That statement alone spoke multitudes to me of this very dynamic. If God is going to act directly, He must have the respect of the others because our prayers are heard and known *by all who serve Him*, and Our Father knows what can be requested and will be respected by the others.

This is what He said:

Pray for freedom.

I will explain why next.

FREEDOM

Our Father told me He can respond in mighty ways for purposes of *protecting* and *defending* the **freedom of His children**. Just as God regards the stewardship of those He has called to serve, He also respects the freedom of His children above everything else.

We are all God's children, and that gives us the birthright to *unlimited potential*. He respects us more than any other part of creation. He said it is His role as a Father *to protect our freedom* and *especially to assist those who want to excel*. Only a loving, democratic God would be so willing and open—so anxious, if you will—for others to succeed.

But this is the God we serve, and He is that way because He is more than God, **HE IS OUR FATHER, and WE ARE HIS CHILDREN**. Some individuals and entities in positions of leadership exert power over others by usurping authority and denying freedoms. Such actions are contrary to the order of God.

We must acknowledge that there are different types of freedom: *political, physical, spiritual, financial, intellectual, emotional, etc.*; an entire book could be written about each one.

The one cause for freedom that Our Father will directly respond to is the *spiritual one.* He said that to get Him to intervene personally; a precise prayer must be prayed. Just as only one key can open a lock, there is only one prayer that will cause God to intervene *directly from His level.* Let me describe in more detail what that means.

1) He cannot intervene on behalf of a people who do not know they are in bondage, and who do not *ask for deliverance.* Such people must work within the timetable and methods as prescribed by those who are in authority over them.

2) The idea must be conceived in the heart or Our Father will not hear it. This includes our dreams at night and our thoughts throughout the day.

3) The intervention must be sought directly from God and not another. He is specifically referring to an intervention by the return of the Lord Jesus Christ. Such an intervention in our day is feasible, but it is Our Father who controls the timing of that event; therefore, it is Our Father to whom we must seek for that intervention.

4) Fourth, is faith. If the prayer is truly conceived in the heart, then there should be enough faith to see it through (that may seem obvious, but it needed to be said). Once oppression has been *realized,* and the prayer from the heart *expressed,* one must have the *faith* to see it through, *however long.*

Now we know some things that must be realized on our end, for Our Father to intervene. Perhaps the hardest task (yet the most essential) *is helping others realize their oppression so that they desire more freedom.*

HOLDING GOD CAPTIVE

As God sits upon His throne, He has been impeded *by our inaction.* At this point in the world's history, all nations have suffered varying degrees of oppression. Part of that is because of superstition, myth, or false traditions.

Our Father made it absolutely clear to me that He will *respect the faith of the living over the prophecies of the dead every time.* Jesus Himself described this when He said: "Let the dead bury their dead" (Luke 9:60). Jesus was referring to those who were *spiritually dead,* giving priority to the *physically dead.* The same could be said of our servitude to false traditions, false interpretations, and dead belief systems.

The spiritually dead have been holding God captive because they are not exercising faith to move Him. When Jesus was upon the earth, He fulfilled many prophecies, *but He also did many new things that were not prophesied.* He did not have to feed the multitudes or the host of other miracles He performed, but He did so because *He respected the needs of the living.*

Today, we have the same rights and the same privileges to do more than what has been prophesied, or that has been done before. In fact, God has promised many times that He will perform a "new work" and Jesus said we are free to "do more" than He did.

18 Remember ye not the former things, neither consider the things of old. Behold, **I will do a new thing**. (Isaiah 43)

12 Verily, verily, I say unto you, He that believeth on me, the works that I do shall he do also; and **greater works than these shall he do**. (John 14)

One verse that seems to perpetuate the idea that God will not do anything new is found in *Ecclesiastes*.

9 The thing that hath been, it is that which shall be; and that which is done is that which shall be done: and **there is no new thing under the sun**. (Ecclesiastes 1)

However, a correct reading of the entire chapter and book shows us that the author is *lamenting the condition of his day, **not endorsing it**.*

14 I have seen all the works that are done under the sun; and, behold, **all is vanity and vexation of spirit**. (Ecclesiastes 1)

In other words, there should always be new things occurring when a faithful people are serving a LIVING God. The types and patterns in the scriptures only tell us what *has been done*, not what will be, unless we let them. We are meant to learn from history, not repeat it. *Our God is a living God, not a computer program.*

The prophecies that have been given can be *abridged, commuted,* **or even** *supplanted.*

We are not bound to them, **neither is God**. In fact, God Our Father wants to be loosed from them, so He can start helping His people **NOW**. How many times does the Bible say, "God repented" of something He had previously said? Many, but only one occurrence is needed to prove that **GOD CAN ALTER A DECREE**. If this were not so, then He would not be *omnipotent*, and there would be no occasion for divine interventions.

The proof that God is a flexible God is demonstrated in the many times that He allowed people to bargain with Him. Whether it was Abraham regarding Sodom (Genesis 18:26-33), or Jesus and the woman from Canaan (Matthew 15:22-28), God is always open to discussion and betterment. All we need is the *right perspective*, the *right prayer*, and *enough faith* to see a new thing through.

This process is how previous great nations attained new heights. *They embraced their day with absolute freedom, and they petitioned God to sustain them.*

CYCLE OF RIGHTEOUSNESS

Throughout the scriptures, there can be what some describe as the "cycle of righteousness." When God's people were doing right, they enjoyed freedom. When they were not, their freedom was taken. Freedom goes hand in hand with God's intervention. When the people suffered enough, and when they conceived in their hearts a desire for freedom, God then heard and answered their prayers; this is also how God can intervene for us now.

Whether it is for a particular group, country, or for the world, if we want God to intervene, there is only one way—the prayer for freedom. Like the key to a lock, it is the prayer of freedom that *SETS GOD FREE.* It is the prayer of freedom that has always been prayed when He has stepped in, and it is the only prayer that He will hear today.

Things CAN be stopped, things CAN be changed, and God CAN intervene, but it must be done THE RIGHT WAY and for the RIGHT REASON. The suffering of humanity could be at its worst, but it is the hindrance to .freedom that concerns Our Father the most.

God IS respectful of freedom, and He will respect the prayers of the righteous for more freedom. Today we are being constrained by paradigms from yesterday. **We have glorified history to the point of worship, sterilized our faith on a pulpit, and banished God to His throne.**

Jesus came to preach "deliverance to the captives" (Isaiah 61:1, Luke 4:18) and He is destined to return. I pray we will include a concern for spiritual injustices, along with our concern for human suffering. I pray we will recognize spiritual oppression wherever it is occurring and not rest until our desire for freedom has brought Heaven to Earth. *Let us therefore pray for intervention—in the name of freedom.*

Then God will respect our prayers and will directly intervene on our behalf. I thank God our Father for answering my prayers, and I thank Him for the teachings given. I pray He will unite those who would like to "Set God Free," with those who like to "Seize the Day," so a new work can be performed like Abraham Lincoln did.

Abraham Lincoln, d. April 15, 1865

In 1865, President Abraham Lincoln signed what would become the **13th Amendment, abolishing slavery in America.** The "Lincoln Memorial" on the western end of the National Mall in Washington, D.C. honors this great man:

Which was further memorialized by the signing of the *Bill of Rights Act of 1964* put forth by Pres. John F. Kennedy:

Martin Luther King Jr. Standing Behind Pres. Johnson as He Signs the Civil Rights Act of 1964

On February 1, 1848, President Harry S. Truman

signed a proclamation designating it *National Freedom Day* in commemoration of the day President Abraham Lincoln signed what would become the 13th Amendment. The inspiration for this came from the work of *Major Richard R. Wright Sr.*

Major Richard R. Wright Sr.

He said:

> "I believe that there should be a day when freedom for all Americans is celebrated. I invite national and local leaders to meet in Philadelphia to formulate plans to set aside **February 1** each year to memorialize the signing of the 13th Amendment to the U.S. Constitution by President Abraham Lincoln on February 1, 1865, which freed all U.S. slaves."[1]

1. See also "February 1 isn't just the start of Black History Month. It's National Freedom day, created by a former slave

His background:

"Richard Robert Wright Sr. (May 16, 1855 – July 2, 1947) was an American military officer, educator and college president, politician, civil rights advocate and banking entrepreneur. Among his many accomplishments, he founded a high school, a college, and a bank. He also **founded the National Freedom Day Association in 1941."** [2]

"The purpose of this holiday is to promote good feelings, harmony, and equal opportunity among all citizens and to remember that the United States is a nation dedicated to the ideal of freedom. Major Richard Robert Wright Sr., **a former slave**, fought to have a day when freedom for all Americans is celebrated. When Wright got his freedom, **he went on to become a successful businessman and community leader** in Philadelphia, Pennsylvania. Major Wright chose February 1 as National Freedom Day because it was the day in 1865 that President Lincoln signed the 13th Amendment to the Constitution."[3]

Honorable men, honorable deeds, and *Memorials of Honor* for the cause of freedom; but there's more to do.

commemorating abolition," *CNN*, https://www.cnn.com/2020/02/01/us/national-freedom-day-richard-wright-trnd/index.html

2. https://en.wikipedia.org/wiki/Richard_R._Wright

3. https://www.americaslibrary.gov/es/pa/es_pa_free_1.html

CHAPTER 12.

FOURTH OF JULY CALLING

I am releasing this title on the 4th of July in commemoration of a meeting I had with Our Lord on the 4th of July years ago. He instructed me to meet Him at a distant campsite, and I arrived on the 3rd and spent the night in fasting and prayer, and on the following day, Jesus took me high above the earth and showed me *His view* of Earth's inhabitants, and in particular His followers.

Fourth of July Meeting Place

Jesus said to me:

> Do you see my followers, and how focused they are on the Antichrist and the prophecies of doom and gloom?

I answered,

> Yes Lord, I can see how they are focused on the Antichrist, and the prophecies regarding doom and gloom.

Jesus then instructed me with these words:

> Tell My people (and all people) to put their faith in Me, and My coming glory, for it will come before the Antichrist—*if he must come.*

Jesus commissioned me to do three things:

1. Correct misplaced faith in the Antichrist.
2. Alert people to His coming glory that will be poured out on the earth, as has been prophesied.
3. Prepare the world for that new light-filled environment.

BONUS CHAPTER - BEVIL

[As a Bonus Chapter I am including "Bevil" which was previously published in Spiritual Journeys – Vol. 3. This testimony begins at the same physical location as events in chapter "Testimony of The Son of God."]

Bevil definition: beat-evil

I was taken today (Saturday, July 22, 2006) high to another mountain to commune with God, for it has been many days that I have been engaged in a project that has kept me cooped up and unable to spend time with our Father outside. He heard my cry and allowed me time to go out.

After driving a great distance, I spotted the glory of God on a hill, shining precisely upon a unique pine tree. It was not a dark green pine, but was much lighter in color, and the branches were spread out.

There was really no place to park except along this country road, so I just trusted my car would not be hit and pulled to the side as far as possible. I got out in my long jeans, shirt, shoes, and hat, took one last swig from my water bottle (leaving it in the car) and headed for the top of that hill, which was atop a mountain of a high elevation.

I was excited to get out and breathe the warm, fresh air. I always enjoy the smell of dry grass and trees in the summer heat, but today was unusually hot, even breaking heat records.

Despite the heat, I pushed myself toward the top but found myself quickly becoming fatigued. I know I am not as young as I once was, but this was unusually hard. I continued to duck underneath the overgrowth going up the hill.

I finally reached the top, yet a distance from the pine tree, which was further along the ridge. And that's when my exhaustion overcame me and passed out. It was so dry, there was no moisture at all. I just kept panting and panting, trying to catch my breath, but it was as if there was no oxygen in that high elevation.

Slowly I was recovering, but wearing those clothes in that heat, without water, wasn't good. I forced myself up and walked along the ridge, pausing under trees for shade as I came to them. There were huge funnel spider webs all along the ground, some five feet in diameter. I had seen nothing like them before. The thought of being bitten by a spider up there was alarming.

Carefully, I continued my journey along the top of the ridge, suffering from the heat with every step. My panting was labored, and I was trying to remain calm, but that was difficult. I finally staggered to the tree, and then the Father told me to lie down and catch my breath.

Desperation had fully set in, mixed with emotions of worry, loneliness, and weakness. I cried out deep in my heart to the Father for help. Suddenly, I detected a most beautiful fragrance which permeated all around me. It smelled like clove plus a few other elements. It was supportive and gave me strength emotionally, which, in turn, calmed me physically.

I hastily cleared an area so I could remove my shirt to lie on and then collapsed, still panting; then I blacked out. Slowly, I came back again, with sweat pouring forth. Then the Savior spoke.

He said He had the formula for which I had asked for years; He understood the need for it. In fact, when I got to that spot on the mountain, the scent that permeated the area was this formula.

He said it was composed of **clove** for its **strength** to **cut through emotions; cinnamon** for its **power** to **warm** and **sustain** clove's strength, **carrying** it into the **stomach** and **soul; frankincense** for the **glory of God** and **presence of Christ**; and **myrrh** for **divinity,** which cuts above all, plus His Spirit.

I wept, for God was good, so good. He brought me here, and I suffered for it, but now I shed tears of comfort and had relief. I was so exhausted it was nearly impossible to praise outwardly, but I gave thanks. All I could do was continue to lie in that spot, in His presence, firm in my love of God.

WATCH

But that was not all, for as soon as the Savior finished His words, a loud screech came from a distance, and then I heard it coming over the hill behind me. Something in the sky was moving at a high rate of speed.

Then the Father said to watch, for:

What you witness, you will be able to do to evil with this formula.

Through the trees in front of me I heard the screech again, and I looked and saw a bird flying quickly, and behind it an enormous bird which swooped down upon it and brought it to the ground.

I was amazed, and instinctively I felt sad and asked the Father, please do not allow a bird to be killed on my behalf. I began to get up, but my strength was spent. The Father said, it will not die, and then I saw the large bird release it, and saw it fly away.

He said to me again:

So too will you be able to do to evil with this formula.

The name "Bevil" then entered my mind as a word suitable for describing what I saw; which is an abbreviation of "beat evil" and rhymes with *weasel*, which is what the devil is.

I rejoice, and have confidence this formula will work, for I have battled evil on its many fronts, and

I know that each of those properties is *precisely* what is needed when things get miserable, cold, evil and scary. And with the added ingredient of God's Spirit, it will be a *Holy Oil.*

Thank you, Father, for allowing the Savior to *minister* to me, for that is what this formula will do for others.

I am confident that as I study these oils, I will find many supporting testimonies of their spiritual and energetic qualities. And I rejoice again that God hears and answers prayers.

PILGRIM SCENT

Some time later, the Lord gave me another formula that He said those in ministry could use daily, which is based on *Warrior Scent,* with the addition of *Rose oil,* and He called it "Pilgrim Scent."

Warrior & Pilgrim Scents

TESTIMONY SERIES

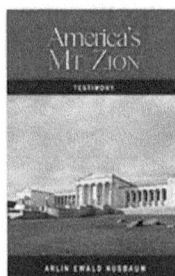

America's
Mt Zion
TESTIMONY
ARLIN EWALD NUSBAUM

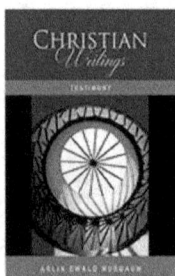

CHRISTIAN
Writings
TESTIMONY
ARLIN EWALD NUSBAUM

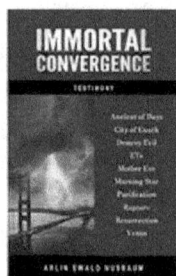

IMMORTAL
CONVERGENCE
TESTIMONY
ARLIN EWALD NUSBAUM

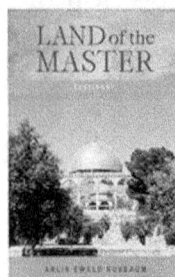

LAND of the
MASTER
TESTIMONY
ARLIN EWALD NUSBAUM

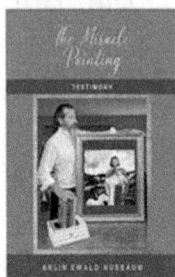

the Miracle
Painting
TESTIMONY
ARLIN EWALD NUSBAUM

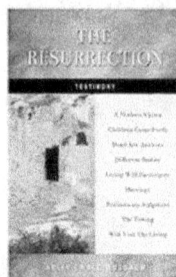

THE
RESURRECTION
TESTIMONY
ARLIN EWALD NUSBAUM

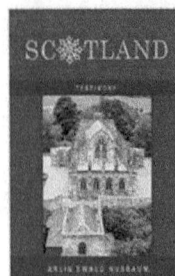

SCOTLAND
TESTIMONY
ARLIN EWALD NUSBAUM

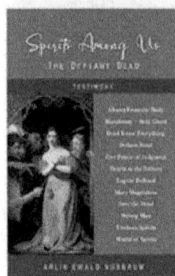

Spirits Among Us
THE DEFIANT DEAD
TESTIMONY
ARLIN EWALD NUSBAUM

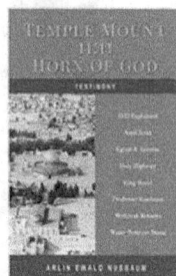

TEMPLE MOUNT
1:13
HORN OF GOD
TESTIMONY
ARLIN EWALD NUSBAUM

ABOUT THE AUTHOR

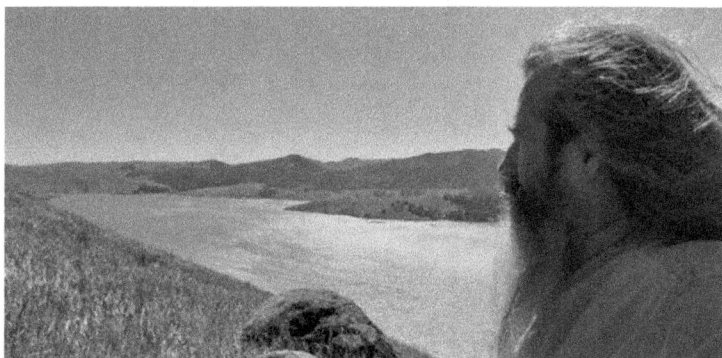

Arlin Ewald Nusbaum

Arlin is happily married and lives with his wife Tammy in San Antonio, Texas. He's the father of seven children and eight grandchildren. He descends from a notable lineage of ministers, including the first martyr under Bloody Queen Mary—the *Rev. John Rogers (1505-1555)*; and other notables including *Sir William Sinclair (1408-1482)* builder of Rosslyn Chapel, *Robert the Bruce (1274-1329)* King of Scots, and *Charlemagne (748-814)*.

Arlin has written about prophecy-related items for three decades and is well-versed in prophetic nuances, including Christianity and Christian unity. He has authored over 100 titles and 30 websites and each one points to *The Millennium of Peace*.

ANM.WORLD